Quarter Life Crisis

Praise for *Quarter Life Crisis*:

Quarter Life Crisis is a Muslim woman's chronology of poems regarding the moral and spiritual dilemmas in the very troubled world around us. In her succinct & explicit showcase of some of humanity's ugliest problems, Bawany evaluates herself and the issues at hand through the lens of the mind, the ego and the soul. As she actively unravels herself into utter vulnerability in the burning world, the reader can't help but to reflect, wrestle, and reconcile with her. This is a poetry collection for activists, for those in spiritual crisis, for those overwhelmed by the world, and for anyone who wants an honest story about heaviness, humility and hope.

- *Amal Kassir, international award-winning spoken word poet*

Sara Bawany's *Quarter Life Crisis* is the perfect poetic salve for any reader. Bawany is inventive and intentional with form as she lays bare not only personal crisis, but the crisis of dying american empire. From faith to family and everywhere in between, Bawany's subject matter is written with compassion and activism at its heart. Bawany is a voice we need in poetry now more than ever.

- *SG Huerta, author of "Last Stop"*

No matter where you open this book, *Quarter Life Crisis* offers a story that's rarely been told before. This is a must-have poetry collection; Bawany's writing is utterly masterful.

- *F.S. Yousaf, bestselling author of "Euphoria", "Serenity", "Prayers of my Youth", and "Sincerely"*

With this rich and storied collection from Sara Bawany, we join the poet in her struggle to balance the weight of youth and adulthood, inheritance and choice, tradition and questions. This beautiful collection carries us from the poet's ancestral homeland and into Texas, bringing forward the voices of her family and their lessons with her, all of it woven together with delicate prayers. Marked with powerful narratives and elegant poetics throughout, Sara's voice emerges with strength and tenderness as she determines toward her own understandings.

- *Suzi Q. Smith, author of "A Gospel of Bones"*

Bawany's voice has evolved with grace, wisdom, and range. Each line is a pulse. Every poem is a living organ. Her latest collection comes alive as a force of greatness. A must-read for young Muslim women seeking to reflect upon their relationship to God, their country, and family.

> - *Marjan Naderi, D.C. Youth Poet Laureate, 7-time poetry slam winner*

Bawany's latest collection of poetry and prose is a powerful soliloquy that is all-encompassing of the themes she explores - a perfect metaphor for what a *Quarter Life Crisis* feels like! This book will have you sitting in awe as the spell-binding words composed by Bawany slam you with a reality that is so raw, yet so beautiful - all at the same time. For readers of all ages, you will not want to put this book down till you reach the last poem. And even then, Bawany leaves you wanting more. Bravo Bawany, this is a masterpiece!

> - *Kashmir Maryam, author of "The Muslim Woman's Manifesto" and "Nafsi"*

Quarter Life Crisis has opened doors for me to think about own my journey through life. Though it is clear Sara draws inspiration from her own experiences, her honest in-mind way of writing compels self-reflection.

> - *Raef Haggag, Singer-Songwriter*

Quarter Life Crisis occupies the crossroads of Bawany's intersectional identities and lenses with which she views the world. Her background as a social worker and activist, her dedication to her faith, and her commitment to art enlivens her to write with momentum, urgency and wisdom . . . As Bawany interrogates her own culture, religion, and upbringing, she ultimately finds her way back to herself, and back to her roots.

> - *Vogue M. Robinson, Clark County, NV Poet Laureate Emerita*

also by Sara Bawany:

(w)holehearted: a collection of poetry and prose

Quarter Life Crisis

Poetry and Prose

Written by: Sara Bawany

Illustrated by: Afeefah Khazi-Syed

FLOWERSONG
PRESS

FlowerSong Press
Copyright © 2023 Sara Bawany
ISBN: 978-1-953447-10-4

Published by FlowerSong Press
in the United States of America
www.flowersongpress.com

Illustrations by Afeefah Khazi-Syed
Cover Photography and Design by
Usama Malik, Sara Bawany and Afeefah Khazi-Syed

Author Contact Information:
Email: bawanysara@gmail.com
Facebook: www.facebook.com/bawany.sara
Instagram: www.instagram.com/sara.bawany
TikTok: www.tiktok.com/sara.bawany

Artist Contact Information:
Afeefah Khazi-Syed: afeefahks@gmail.com
Usama Malik: usama.malik2173@gmail.com

NOTICE: SCHOOLS AND BUSINESSES
FlowerSong Press offers copies of this book at quantity discount with
bulk purchase for educational, business, or sales promotional use. For
information, please email the Publisher at info@flowersongpress.com.

In the name of God, the Most Merciful,
the Most Compassionate.

"So where are you going?"
- Qur'an, 81:26

*My mission is to turn stories of suffering
into narratives of healing.*

Table of Contents

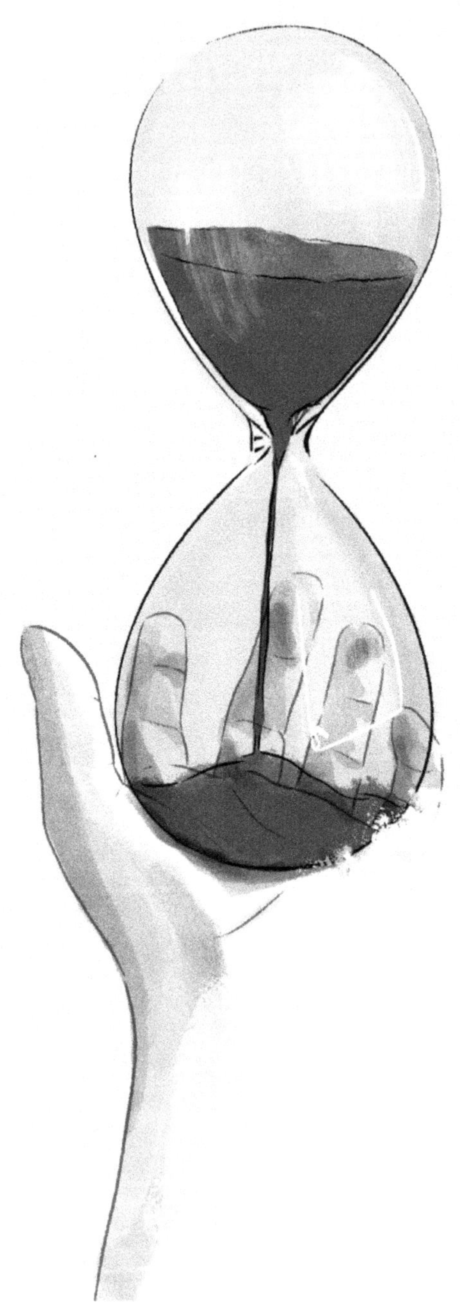

Birthday Surprises Pt. I

The day I turned 13, I decided to start keeping a journal to write to my future self, so that one day I could look back on it and see how far I had come. I decided to reread it before I started my first big-girl job. 219 entries over the span of 10 years and I couldn't put my own story down. I watched a spunky little girl go to four different middle schools at perhaps one of the most important times in an adolescent's life. I watched her deal with her parents' divorce, cry about boys, and have her spirit broken by her friends over and over.

I want to go back in time and tell that 13-year-old girl that putting on the hijab in a town with few Muslim inhabitants other than her family was so much braver than she realized. I want the 15-year-old version to know that the reason for her constant self-doubt and high-strung nerves was because of the anxiety and depression she'd be diagnosed with much later. I want to beg the 17-year-old girl to not lose the fire in her heart. To stay feisty. To not retreat into her shell when people she trusted continued to hurt her. To keep being the person who could strike up a conversation with any stranger. To not fret about not having the perfect body. To accept the color of her skin and love herself for it. I want to shake the 19-year-old version of her by the shoulders and scream that God would never abandon her. Tell her not to stress about the future so much. Tell her gently that she isn't as mature as she thought but that she would get there one day.

I want to hug every single version and tell them hey, don't you worry. Because you're going to grow up to be a poet, a leader, and an artist. You're going to learn how to bake cookies perfectly after years of trying and your poems will make people cry and heal. 90% of the friends who hurt you will come back and apologize, and you will have a client sitting in your office thanking you for helping turn her life around, only a few years after you believed you were a failure for not pursuing the career you spent years planning for. It will be fine. You will be fine.

You will be just fine.

The Motherland

has been awaiting my return,
and after 17 years, I crossed the ocean to make the journey
home.

I dreamed of the day she would welcome me with frail arms
and how I would weep at her feet.
I always imagined myself as that child of diaspora
who would inhale the fragrance of the dirt,
falling in love with her many flaws,
and I anxiously counted down the days
until we would be reunited.

But when I stepped off the plane,
she was beyond recognition.

Didn't match the description or the pictures
my parents had lamented over
throughout the years.

Her scent was pungent and unbearable,
smog startling my eyes with tears.
Garbage and beggars with missing
limbs lined her streets.

There was no pleasant surprise,
only a mockery of what she was.
All the parts I thought I would love about
her had atrophied away into oblivion

and the men in the streets ogled me
as I searched in my broken mother tongue
for any remnants I could salvage.

I now find myself lodged in the liminal space
between two vastly different worlds.

This one is nothing like I had dreamed of,
while the one I now call "home" played a role
in her demise.

The bridge between both has long decayed.
Which side of the crevice, then,
shall I climb out of?

For Dark-Skinned Girls

When we were children, brown or black
      used to be another way to say burnt,
and burnt was another way to say ugly.

      Our mamas would slather Fair & Lovely
across our little faces in hopes that it
      would sting just enough to peel strips

of melanin right off. They didn't know better, I suppose,
      cursing their DNA, trying to save us from the fate
generations before them suffered. But now,

      now we know better. This skin we've tried
so hard to shed serves as a testament
      to how much the sun found home in us, how

it is the darkest soil that grows the most vibrant
      flowers, how it is the night sky that holds the
universe's greatest secrets. And if God

      lovingly grabbed handfuls of the fertile
soil and pieces of the night sky to
      fashion our skin, how dare you call us

ugly?

Nodus Tollens

I can't put my finger on this feeling.
"Frustration" is all too easy a word
but "loss of control" gnaws at the tip
of my tongue like a bruise.

The therapist asks me where in my body
I feel this and I don't know how to explain
that it's everywhere and nowhere
and somewhere else all at the same time.

I can pinpoint "fear" now at the base
of my throat where I swallow over and over
as if repeating the same motions will
get me used to the dread, and the routine
which is so mundane I want to escape.

And this life threatens
to break itself over
my back while all I ask
for is answers.

Uncles Of Palestine

The uncles of Palestine are a different breed of men. They can spot newcomers from one end of Jerusalem to another. With a warm smile, they ask if you need help. Where you are going. Where you are from. Give you precise directions. They know many can't return there. They welcome you to the Holy Land anyway.

The uncles of Palestine laugh heartily. Cigarettes in one hand and shai in the other, they speak of their families and of current events. They delight in a foreigner who can chat in broken Arabic with them and they sell olives and spices and pomegranate juice in the alleyways of the old city. Knafeh doesn't taste the same anywhere else and they know this well, insisting on taking you to the best bakery in Jerusalem.

The uncles of Palestine are a Godsend. The ones who safeguard the holy sites and are eager to teach you the history of the sacred earth beneath your feet. The shopkeepers with their bushy mustaches and kind eyes who tell you stories of apartheid. The bus drivers, their generosity having no bounds, who send money home to their families, but can't return to them. The taxi drivers who have transported travelers from around the world. The ones who turn from drivers to safeguards. The ones who turn from workers to friends.

The uncles of Palestine, in their gentle and patient demeanor, and in their quick wits and sharp tongues, are the definition of resistance. They ignore the implanted soldiers at the gates and walk to Al-Aqsa every morning for Fajr. The way they live. The way they love. The fire in their eyes. The tranquility shining through their smiles is enough to make you fall in love with this land. This keeper of the olive trees. This home of the prophets.

Muzzle

When I say
        I like that my clients cry in my office
What I mean is
        I am thankful they found a place
        outside their façade of steel
        where they can place their dignity at my feet
        and be vulnerable.

When I say
        I don't know what to do
        when grown men are the ones
        crying in my office
What I mean is
        their need to profusely ask forgiveness
        for unloading their baggage on me
        is them stripping themselves of the masks
        they were never meant to wear in the first place
        and apologizing for it.

Crying is still perceived as a weakness
but to drop the shell in one go and ask for help
is like successfully pulling sword from stone.

Ode To The Nutella Cortado

I'm not really a coffee drinker but a Nutella cortado once
      surged its way into my bloodstream and carved the anger

      and poem out with a vengeance (disclaimer: I didn't know
what a cortado was but I saw the word Nutella and got

excited, thought, how could this not be good and I was half
      right it was the most disgusting thing I'd ever tried) but it

      unearthed the magic hidden beneath my rage my fingers
hammered away at my keyboard at 1 a.m. so riled up I

swear the entire house was humming that night and trust
      me I'm not a night owl (anymore) but I guarantee I felt it my

      heart was galloping so fast I thought it would barrel right
out of my mouth any second and it did in the form of the

best poem I had ever unleashed now I jokingly call myself
      a recreational coffee drinker but what I really mean is that

      there is a gentle hurricane submerged somewhere deep
inside me and I know just the thing to gradually coax it out

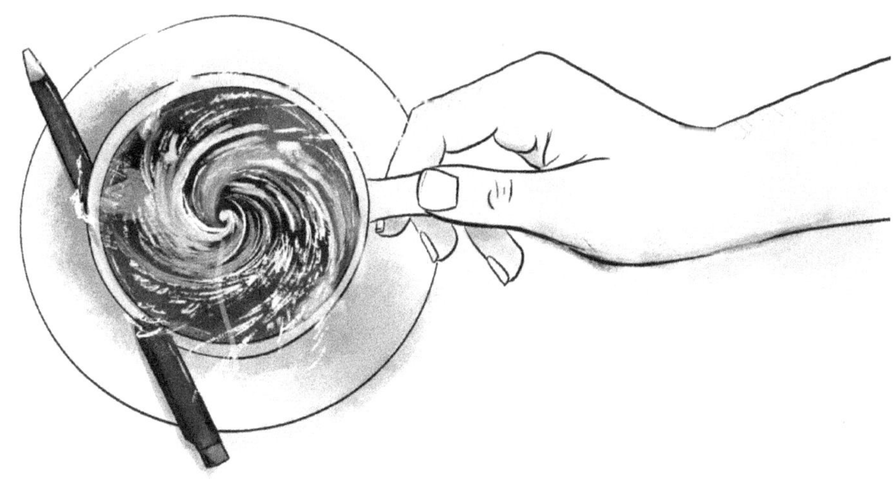

Unraveling

When I was coming of age
    with a freshly rejuvenated
        sense of spirituality
            I felt God speak to me –
                told me that the way I
                    could be closest to Him
                        was to rid my life of sinners
                            (and as a byproduct, men).

                                            I listened.

I felt God tell me
    that to be completely faithful
        I must make people uncomfortable
            with the truth
                even if it meant
                    putting myself
                        in danger.

                                            I listened.

When the devil finally spoke
    it was then I realized it had been
        his voice all along
            that my understanding of God
                had always been far beyond my capability
                    that my arrogance had tricked me
                        into believing that cutting
                            myself off was

                                            the answer.

It was then
    that I had wound myself up
        so tight in my "sincerity"
            I was in the perfect position to

                                            snap.

So when the devil
    commanded me
        to sever all ties with myself
            I unraveled and unraveled
                all the way

                                            into his arms.

        I have been trying to find my way back ever since.

Garden Seventeen

Every Ramadan, my period arrives at the most inconvenient time.
Sometimes twice – the second one an especially unwelcome guest
often lingering long enough to overstay its visit.

This year, amidst re-discovering iftar parties post-pandemic,
it is four days late.
The cramps have gnawed at me for weeks and I wonder at the delay.

During the scorch of a typical Texas afternoon
while I am exploring a plant shop,
a place I am convinced is a snippet
of what heaven must be like,
my stomach rumbles loudly
and beads of sweat start to form at my temple.

When I arrive home drenched
and see the blood,
I am quiet for a minute.

Instead of throwing my head up in angst
that a day of fasting is wasted,
grumbling and taking notes about
how many more fasts I now need to make up,
I laugh with absolute delight for the first time.

What other explanation could there be
except that the growl of my stomach must have
reached the heavens!
God must have looked down upon me
standing next to the jasmine plants,
stuck in a feverish daydream
about the size of Jannah's trees,
and taken pity,
must have commanded my body
to let me eat and drink an hour before everyone else.

So instead of anger,
I quietly look up,
drink in the water from the cool shower,
and whisper, *thank you.*

The path of least resistance,
the one that reminds me of God's infinite mercy –
that is the one I want to find myself on.

Mamma,

do you remember that time
you persistently asked for permission
to make and sell your
flower arrangements
at the masjid bazaar?

I can still envision you sitting
on the floor of our dining room
hours into the night,
pliers and bits of green
foam and fake roses
buried in the carpet
as you labored away.

Not a single person bought them.

I remember how dejected you were.
Felt the hurt somewhere deep in my belly.

But where do you think I learned
how to stand up on a mic
trembling and reading experimental poems
too fast for anyone to understand
if I didn't think they would later
blossom?

Ode To The New Hijabi In School

"Asalaamu'alaikum" feels weird to say here, doesn't it?
Let's just stick with, "Salaam girl so where are you from?"
Do you wanna ask the teacher where you and I
can pray Dhuhr together in the middle of lunch?

Chiffon or satin or viscose or modal?
Pins or no pins? Under cap or no?
How do you drape it so perfectly?
Will you give me a tutorial after class?
By the way, that salad at lunch has bits of bacon in it;
be careful.

Have you seen that brown boy with the nice beard across the hall?
Do you think he's "Muslim Muslim" or "wallah bro Muslim?"
He plays basketball at the masjid every Friday night, but I saw him
holding hands with that girl over there so probably the latter.
Astaghfirullah that's gross –
she's not even pretty, she's just white.

Let's break our fast together at the pep rally.
I already have a hundred in this class, but we get extra credit for going.
Do your parents not let you stay out late or listen to music either?
Which masjid do you spend Ramadan at?

Anyway, the boys keep asking me why we wear this thing on our heads
and if Osama was our grandfather.
How much you wanna bet we'd be suspended
if we actually said yes?

Us feisty girls, wrapped in elaborately pinned scarves
that can't hide the mouth on us,
designated experts on all things math, curry and terrorism.

Someone asked me the other day if you and I are related to each other,
even though we speak different languages
and have tremendously distinct complexions.

We might as well be.

We're the only ones who understand what it means
to be so radiant that no one around us notices.

Subhan'Allah.

Quarantine Meditation

We reconnected in the middle of a tempest.
Your compassion had been outstretched toward us for ages
and it was only when our hearts were in our throats
that we felt our jugular veins pulsing.
You have always been there – we were just too comfortable to notice.

And here You are,
entire worlds being shifted in an upheaval of reality.
The storms we created have finally ravaged our shores.
We are either calling out Your name
or in the process of abandoning it.

You have humbled the inhabitants of this world
while the pharaohs of it continue to drown themselves in denial.
You have offered us Your mercy to redeem us of our purgatory while
the monsters of this vast sea climb upon our backs in attempts to surface.
But they don't – we are all drowning "equally" for once.

And it is the unsung heroes who have channeled the
power of hope You have reminded us about all along.
That in between the pockets of anxiety there is an outpouring of love.
That joining hands in this storm can build the most powerful bridges.
After all a people united with You on their side can never truly fall.

And the world continued to hope. The people continued to sing
outside their windows. Loved ones felt closer across the room
than ever before. And You flipped the universe on its head.
Those who were ignored became heroes.
The true faces of kings were revealed.

And the people couldn't come out
but the sun finally did.
and soon,
by Your grace,
so shall we.

Birthday Surprises Pt. II

Every year on October 22nd, I can be found in a quiet state of reflection. Today, I am contemplating pages and pages of journal entries typed out by 13-year-old hands. My lips may smile and tell you how great it is to be however old I am that year —

but my mind is back to June 2008 during the biggest chasm of my life. It is back to October 2014 when I finally understood that I wasn't meant to be what I thought, but something else just as great. It is apprehensively reflecting on January 2017 when I discovered that I didn't want to be alive anymore.

And then I come rushing back to now, marveling at the fact that I am ever more aware of my body and my youth slowly slipping away.

Age really is just a number, and I've always been privileged enough to believe that. But I must recognize that I can't be the superhero I was at 16. I must admittedly forgive myself for really starting to need those 8 hours of sleep. And I must acknowledge that I feel the very slight pangs of decline even now in my mid-twenties.

Though I've struggled my whole life to celebrate my mere existence when there is always so much more to focus on, today, I am simply – and surprisingly – grateful for it.

Vacancy

How do two people

build a foundation together

at the base of each other's throats

exchanging tools of wisdom –

a reverberation of promises

and dropped hammers

concluding with a handiwork masterpiece

and then part ways suddenly

becoming strangers

What happens to the photographs

plastered behind their eyelids

as a glimpse into each other's world

do they disappear into the attic

along with the relationship

never to be seen again

what happens to the groundwork

does it await the owners that built it

does the concrete cave in

does it demolish itself from the inside out

waiting

waiting

waiting

waiting

Things I Say To Convince Myself I'm Not A Poet

The best artists are "wild and free
spirited" but I am too crispy too
rigid too much of a straight edge
so I must not be a poet not enough
of a rule breaker the most unexpected
loudmouth but only in my head and
sometimes online enamored with
ritual but not enough on leaning
into the chaos that is my obsessively
organized life all my poems are typed
in the Notes app and I want to throw
handwritten pieces across the room
because I can never decipher what
they say that's how bad my handwriting
is how ironic to never lose anything but
to lose entire poems because of how I
wrote them down so I guess I'm not a real
poet my brain is always on fire I don't have
the ability to slow down my mind moves
too fast for my fingers to keep up journaling
which saved my life at one time now feels
fruitless I brave the words enough to get
up on the mic but I speak so fast no one
understands them I've dipped my toes into
four different languages but my metaphors
are often crumbling before they even begin
to take shape I have 400 books on my book
shelf and I haven't read but a third of them
doesn't that make me a fraud I'm content
with the staircase to hell my mind is going
down what does it take to find the poem
in the air and catch it and hold on
to it for dear life can someone more
qualified please remind me?

The Dilator

When the bloodstain first appeared
I was 11 years old
and it was the summer before sixth grade.
I cried harder than I ever had in my life.
The old soul that everyone told me I was
knew even then that the pains of womanhood
were not made easy by this world,
that everything was about to change.

Fast forward 13 years
and my nagging feeling that something
is not quite right down there intensifies.
It is only during my first attempted pap smear
when the doctor touches me and I scream in pain
that my harrowing suspicions are confirmed.

My body has betrayed me,
I keep telling myself.
It's a punishment for my sins,
I guess wildly.

The biology of a woman tells me this shouldn't be real
but as I lay for months after on the bathroom floor
straining to create what should have already existed,
the hole grows wider and my confusion does too.

How can thousands of women be living with this?
Is the lady who bags my groceries one of them?
Is it my neighbor with no children?
Have I ever passed her on the street?
And would the shame be easier to carry
if we could each hold up a corner?

Our bodies did not betray us.
Instead the collective disgrace
ironically commanded our restraint
as did the rapes
and the tears
and the secrecy
and the silence
and the silence
and and and
and and and
and and and

Quarantine Day #121

The hurricane makes landfall
in the border towns of Texas.

Hit hard with mass death
by this silent killer of a virus,

flooded psyches now wrestle
with the rising waters.

Two hundred miles north,
a rainbow bursts out of the sky

amidst the shadowy rolling
threatening rain clouds.

Awestruck, I speed down the empty
highway in a very curated rebellion,

but the rainbow's appearance
ushers me toward a privileged relief.

How peculiar that at the outskirts
of the destruction of this storm

in this near parallel universe,
we have the luxury to revel in rainbows.

Alternate Response To Coercion

When he won't listen to your "no," and still
craves your lips for himself though you never
belonged to him,

submerge your mouth into the depths of
hell. Emerge

holding burning coals between your
teeth, your tongue a charred remnant of
your voice,

the acrid smell of burnt flesh dripping
off your jaw.

Does he still want to kiss you now?

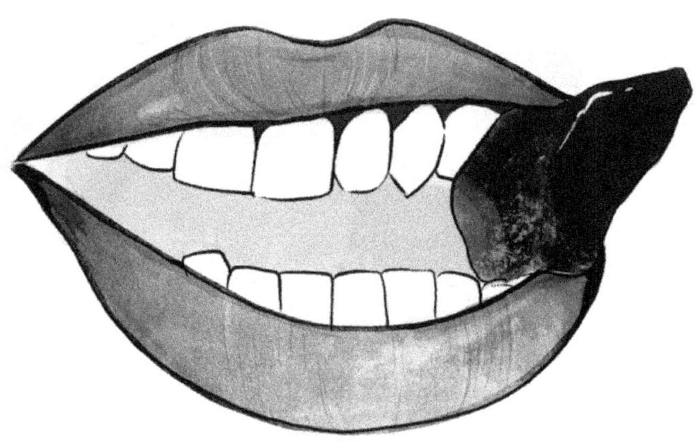

Terrible 2(0)s

It shows up differently now. It wears a new mask and has a different odor but it has been the same entity all along. How did you think you were finally rid of it. When like you, it had just matured into its final form. It has prevented you from observing the solitude of a sunrise for three years. The heat of it is unbearable as is the act of witnessing so many people suffering and you are suffering knowing they are suffering. Your despair is stronger and more desperate; you could learn a thing or two about faith from your younger self. You don't remember what it's like to pray with a sound heart and clear mind. You check your bank account constantly just to make sure every penny you earned is still there. Your nightmares about abandonment have turned into dreaming of tasks you can never complete. About emails you have been waiting to receive. How could you have been so naive. So as to not recognize it for years. Your hand has been around your own throat and you have been confused as to who is choking you. You are always hungry for something and can never figure out what. Your hair is falling out in clumps as if even your body is dying to escape itself. Life is passing you by and you are just fighting to take one breath at a time. You have come to understand that you have a difficult time journaling and praying and crying for the same reason – you are afraid that once you start, you will never be able to stop. It has morphed from self-hatred into a genuine fear for everyone around you. It has morphed into a resentment so deep all the therapy in the world can't get rid of it. You are exhausted all the time and now you know why. You don't want to live in a world with this monster or all the monsters that have birthed this one. You contemplate the bottle of sleeping pills in your nightstand for half a second wondering at the magnitude of this loneliness you know can't possibly be real. You want to tell them this the day you accidentally down them. Engrave it into your headstone. Tell them about how God and the desire to feel at peace felt so far away that all you wanted was to be closer. Forgive yourself for the way it ended. You'd rather not be here than have to witness the battle of your body fighting to keep itself together. Forgive yourself for believing that the only way to take back your power was to take it away from anyone else who could destroy you first.

Reckoning

God has told us that the prayers
of the oppressed
are never forsaken.
It is promised that a mother's dua'a
does not go unanswered.

I can only conclude
that the prayers of women
who have been kept under
the feet of authority
for generations,
cracked hands supplicating endlessly
as they prepare food
for husbands, children,
their own oppressors,
will be answered with a fervor
God is saving for the afterlife.

The chains that shackle their tongues
will one day testify lovingly in their name.
Centuries of silence
and thirsty patience
will be no more.

Their oppressors,
who don't just carry mustard seeds
of arrogance
within their hearts,
but are overflowing with bushels of it,
will one day have to answer for their crimes.

Blaming the feminists,
the women who have devoted their lives
to destroying the very power structures
they grew up adoring,
will be laughable
on a day where the justice
that was never possible in this world
will be handed out

equally.

One Of My Clients Died

Instagram story of a yearbook photo:
eight-year-old child with missing front teeth
in a smile all too familiar.
Eyes that pierced through you even back then.

Why are you here?
What brought you to
therapy?

A Facebook janazah announcement:
Inna lillahi wa inna ilayhi raji'oon
all over my timeline. I keep scrolling
through the comments, but I can't outpace
my own tears, falling thick and heavy.

I just really want to do better
with my life. I've made a lot
of mistakes.

Shoulders shaking with grief,
I pull up my old case spreadsheet,
squinting through the blur to find
his name. There, beside it,
the note dating a year back says:
"Client will call later."

I hurt a lot of people. [   ]
got me down pretty bad.

Even after death, some rules must remain.
So it feels wrong to reveal why I cry for him.
What does confidentiality really mean
when he's reached his end?

I have a job now. I work at
my [   ]'s [   ].
It's going pretty great. I
can buy myself a car soon.

To mourn for someone you know is easy.
But to mourn for someone silently
means to simultaneously carry
case files and an obituary on your shoulders,
disallowing yourself from sharing the grief.

If we could have that final session,
I would tell him
to remember his mother's smile,
to cherish his time with family.

I would tell him to love with his full heart,
to dismantle all the regrets
and to take a chance with God,
since he'd be meeting Him
very soon.

Transitions

Time moves fast these days. Lately, work consists of a lot
of changes. I packed up my office after two years and took down
the photo wall that enchanted so many visitors.
Framed diplomas, books and my treasured salt rock lamp
disappeared from their stations as I removed every trace
of what made this space mine.

The room is bare now.

Transitions are necessary, I tell myself firmly,
no matter how painful they may seem.

Speaking up is also necessary, despite the anxiety that grips
my throat (in my case, fingers). But I have promised
to write my way to truth, whatever that looks like. Today,
it feels a step closer. Today, it looks like making a choice
to leave. Today, the grip I hold over myself is receding.

Oddly enough, even that is painful.

Quarter Life Crisis

My whole life, I've been told
that my name Sara means "princess."
Babynames.com further defines it as
"joy" and "delight," but also "noblewoman,"
"lady of high rank."

I'm severely anti-classist so I find this to be outrageous.

I like everything to be symmetrical, but
I have trouble parking straight. My love
language is "words of affirmation," and as a poet,
the irony isn't lost on me. The first boy I loved
told me I was a "dumb genius,"
so clearly I am an amalgam of paradoxes.

My birthplace is Minnesota, but I hate the cold. I was born
in October, but my favorite season is spring. I'm loud
around quiet people and quiet around loud people. Gryffindor –
the Hogwarts house known for bravery – is where I get sorted
into by every quiz I have ever taken, but my anxiety
cripples me daily.

The MBTI test says I'm an INFJ – or "the counselor."
The Enneagram says I'm a 1 – or "the reformer."
And the phrase my therapist told me years ago, about
how I'm 16 going on 40, is finally starting to make sense.

The flowers on my bedside are currently decaying, and isn't that
the metaphor for our mid-twenties? How a thing that ought to be
blooming is just not?

My diary tells me that at the age of 14,
I could start a conversation with a stranger, but
today, I can't walk into a room full of people
I don't know without having a meltdown. I spent years
trying to force myself to feel safe in this body,
but somewhere along the way, the little brown girl
who always ended up top of her class amongst an endless sea
of white faces began to internalize:
If I'm not the best one in the room,
then I have nothing to offer.
I am nothing.
Somewhere along the way, that began to feel true.

I traversed 11 different schools in my life, so the idea of permanence
was a fantasy. I learned from a very young age
that home was wherever I was. So I've kept
all my goodbye cards, funny homework assignments,
art projects, and my first actual poetry book held together by staples
inside a three-piece set of memory boxes. Because after being uprooted
so many times, these were all I had left.

My beloved tells me that when he holds me,
only half of me is in his arms, and the other half
is looking around for something in the room to straighten
or clean. My job description includes teaching others
how to calm their anxiety, but I myself don't know
how to stop searching for something else to fix, and I will scrub
my hands raw to disguise the chaos inside. There is a history
of OCD in my family, and I suspect history
is repeating itself.

Hi –
my name is Sara.
I'm a social worker, a therapist, and a poet.
I love Nutella and Talenti gelato.
I'm also severely flat-footed and trip on everything in sight.

My hobbies include:
drowning in nostalgia,
collecting poetry books,
and beating myself up over things I can't control.

I'm a master at organizing my possessions, and I rarely
lose things, but sometimes I wonder if I've lost myself
trying to fix everything around me.

I guess no matter how much I try to organize my life,
no matter how many tasks I take on
and how many checklists I create,
I am procrastinating
how much work is left to do
just to learn
to love
myself.

The Photograph

She flips through
an old family photo album,
yellowing pages
with faded pictures,
points out different family members
and introduces me to her early years.

She turns to a page and stops.
The air suddenly feels heavier.
This man, she points,
molested me and my cousin
when we were little girls.
My breath catches
at the flatness of her voice,
the steel in her eye.

I ask why he's still in the album.
She tells me her family might reprimand her
if they notice its disappearance,
despite knowing how he violated her.
Besides, he's dead anyway.
I hold out my hand firmly
and ask her for the photograph,
family be damned.
She looks almost relieved
as she pulls the thin paper out
from between the plastic slip.

Later, at the gas station,
I stand by the trash can
and rip the photo in half,
and then in fourths,
and then in eighths.
I keep going.
I am aware
of the man at the next pump
watching me curiously,
and I do not care
I do not care
I do not care
I do not care
I do not care
I do not care

A Response To: "You're A Little Too Radical"

Yes because the dirt that crumbles between our fingers has not yet dried from all the blood that was spilled to fulfill manifest destiny / because despite all the work there are days the mirror cackles at my unruly curls and dark skin / because July 4th is a cacophony of fireworks raining down from the night sky to muffle the cacophony of bombs raining down back home / because billionaires could eradicate world hunger but are instead eating us alive with greed only to dehydrate themselves in space / because the decayed bones of children are begging to be unearthed / because the Global South dared to defy gravity and was forced to orbit a celestial body it had vowed never to bow down to / because prophets were also considered "too radical" / because the Middle Passage was the most unwilling graveyard to ever exist where nobody was dignified with a funeral / because the people who claim to represent us screech at the sight of pigs but still scavenge for photo ops with them / because mother earth is being strangled by lined pockets and empty hearts / because a book store owner mourns his life's work knowing he can no longer bring smiles to the people of Gaza / because a publicly known rapist just gave a grandiose speech at a wedding / because your favorite sheikh is fondling little boys and girls / because slavery is now concealed behind bars / because the man who beats his wife is the spitting image of the man who writes policies to tear families apart / because some of us still believe that the entities dripping of flesh at their jaws are coming to save us / because all of this is the true violence they keep distracting you from / because every single oppression is interconnected and there is so much work to be done / because this world feels so evil some days that I am positive God's greatest mercy to mankind was creating hell.
//
Call me radical because I don't know how to live in this world without that fire / because this rage feels like I am about to burn it all down / because I dream of the day we can build a new world from the ashes / because I swear there is no other way to be / because it is the only way to be.

End Of Days

Smiling in the face of the atrocities
rising up around me
feels selfish.
If I can't save the world,
or if God has some other plan
for my endless prayers,
then perhaps squashing
whatever joy I have left
should do the trick.

This is the beginning
of the end of times they spoke about.
These are the stories I grew up hearing
from parents and Sunday school teachers.
The widespread corruption,
the Earth swallowing itself whole,
and a deep desire from the most privileged
to hold on so desperately
to the cruel world they've built,
the only heaven they will likely ever know.

I waver between resigning to hopelessness
and refusing to accept defeat.
The world is burning itself to hell.
Mothers are being forced
to give up their womanhood,
unable to feed their children,
burying their sons,
watching fires hungrily
gorge on their homes.
What luxury did I deserve
to not be the one in their place
or they be in mine.

But here I am,
unable to move or leave my bed.
To feel so weighed down by grief
that to know what must be done
and being unable to do it
is a slap in the face to those who are still fighting.
I've always thought of myself as a warrior,
as courageous,
but how on earth do I fight injustice
when I can't even fight my own demons?

Imam Hussain taught us
with his last breath
that it is prophetic to fight
until our own.
It is our courage
in the face of something impossible
that matters at the end,
and if this is truly the end
I shall brace myself for
the war and conclude
in the face of multiple apocalypses
that it's time to take our pick
of which way we want to go out.
So that when God asks us on the final day
what we did in this time of suffering,
what we did to make this world better
before we left it,
we will finally
have
answers.

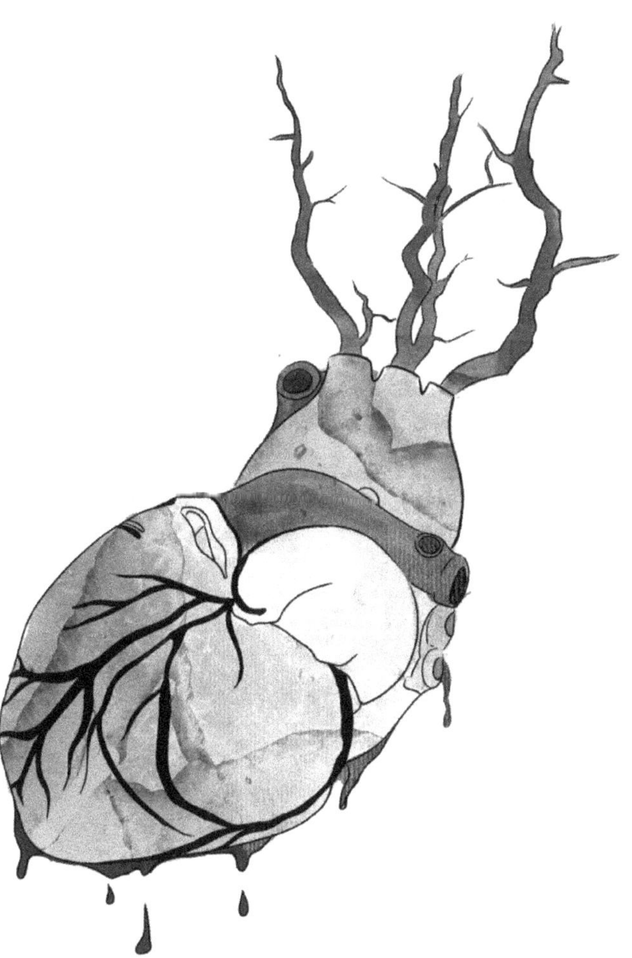

To Religious People Who Don't Believe In Activism

Do you think your faith was handed to you on a silver platter?
That your prophet curtsied his way down from heaven
with a holy book tucked beneath his arm?
How incredible that you recite origin stories
with an iron tongue
but if God was really on your mind,
would it choke on its own ignorance?

Yes, your religion is one of peace,
but it birthed itself into this world and waged
an entire revolution to keep itself grounded.
And here you are. Thousands of miles away
from its womb claiming that protesting and politics
will take us to hell.
If your ancestors hadn't sacrificed themselves for your faith,
I guess you certainly would have ended up there.

Faith is not a series of words uttered in a particular order
in prayer as much as it is the heart that beats with God's justice
blooming from beneath its tongue.
Faith is not being an expert in Latin and Arabic
as much as it is being a master of the universal language of kindness.
Faith is in the eye that cries
for forgiveness as much as it is the hand that tears down
the walls of hatred in its own home.
After all, God says in the Qur'an
that He won't change a people until
they change themselves.
God didn't say He won't change a people
unless they prayed hard enough.

One of our most beloved stories
is that of Abraham smashing all the idols and then blaming the biggest one,
but civil disobedience is just a little too radical for us.
We'll cheer on Moses for facing off with the pharaoh,
but then have lunch with our oppressors in a heartbeat
for the sake of "dialogue" (spoiler alert –
we are not at the table; we are on the menu).
We revere Jesus for speaking truth to power in favor of the poor,
but Jesus didn't consider it "charity."
Jesus didn't post it to social media.
Jesus didn't step outside his own comfortable bubble
to help the less fortunate. Rather,
Jesus was part of the community he helped create change in.

Prophet Muhammad held secret meetings, wrote letters
to kings, taught his people how to pray behind closed doors,
escaped assassins, resisted a boycott, built an army, was commanded
by God to fight, made peace treaties, saved female children
from being buried alive, enacted new laws, bloodlessly
conquered a whole city.

Here's a radical idea: all of our prophets were divinely guided
activists. All of our prophets lived and breathed revolution.
Words like "activism" and "prophet" are in need
of their own revolution.
Because if activists can be educators and doctors and writers
and poets and mothers and children, and if prophets were also shepherds
and kings and carpenters and fugitives and prisoners and people –

What I mean to say is,
if the way the prophets lived their lives
was meant to be the real message,
how well are we receiving it?

History lesson: The first men of Islam knew how to cry.
It was the softness of their hearts which enabled them to be the fiercest
warriors this world has ever seen. And they were not afraid of death
because they were better than that.

History lesson: One of the first converts to Islam was a child
who later grew up to be a soldier, a leader, and a khalifa,
known for fiercely radical policies but egalitarian treatment of people.
Imagine if he decided he would rather hide at home and pray.

History lesson: The first person to die for Islam was a poor, Black woman.
She was tortured to death for her beliefs. She sacrificed her body,
was torn limb from limb, and is honored today as a martyr.

So as you sit idly in your comfortable home
or in the ivory tower criticizing the protestors
on your expensive television set,
gold-plated Qur'an verses adorning
your walls, tell me again
how you don't believe in activism.

0

when i was in 8th grade, the court ordered a psychological evaluation on us in
the midst of a messy divorce. i was 95 pounds attending my 9th school & felt
16 different ways about this. i found the 104-page report years later. amongst

all the psychologist got right (& all he got wrong) he declared that my journal
entries indicated an odd fixation on food & clothing. how could it not?
maslow's hierarchy, while flawed, states that without our basic needs – food,

water, shelter & safety – being met, it's unlikely for us to reach the upper 4
stages. but the psychologist left out the part about money. how at the age of
13, i noted that a can of sprite was a preposterous $3.50. that when people i

loved bestowed me with gifts, the first thing i asked was how much it cost
them. at 7, my parents said money was tight & i couldn't have things i wanted,
so naturally i stopped asking for things i needed. at 9, i developed a habit of

counting letters in nearly every word & sentence i heard and then dividing
them into multiples of 3. math was always my best subject so maybe i ended
up in the wrong field & i know it sounds silly because the doctors said i was

okay, but look how well i count when i am positive that no matter how many
times i divide a number i will never end up with 0. & i've decided that maslow
got it 100% wrong. it's not just that you can't reach the upper stages but once

you've tasted scarcity at the bottom your guilt will overtake you no matter
how high up you go. why else do our immigrant parents balk at our "luxury"
purchases? as the youngest student in my graduate program at 20, the $31,000

of student loans reared its head toward me & the scarcity disfigured my moral
compass: here's a corner i can cut. here's a bit i can take if no one's watching.
always the good honest girl now mooching off next door's wi-fi & laundry.

how much can i make off these textbooks at the end of the semester. here,
take my clothes, whatever little assets i own. here's a moldy old rug i can make
a few pennies from. my items were no longer possessions, they were the

difference between making rent & ending up a failure. work night shifts at a
desk job so i can do my homework & walk home at 4 am? no problem as long
as my electricity won't be cut off. uber drive home the passenger who has

placed his hand on my thigh? i grit my teeth & imagine kicking him out of this
rickety old car with no shoes or phone, but the trip will increase me 56 dollars
so tell me, what else is there to lose & the answer is everything everything

everything.

Ho(lie)r Than Thou

"Allah does not like the public mention of evil except by one who has been
wronged. And ever is Allah, Hearing and Knowing."
- Qur'an 4:148

"There is no blame on those who enforce justice after being wronged. The
blame is only against the ones who wrong the people and tyrannize upon
the earth without right. Those will have a painful punishment."
- Qur'an 42:41-42

I once read that the percentage of narcissists is higher in
religious leadership positions than it is in the general population.
It makes sense, doesn't it?
If God has forbidden taking partners with Him, the only way
they'd bypass that would be to just decide they are God.

When rows and pews and upturned palms begin to feel heavier,
confessionals disintegrate into dust.
Somewhere secluded, his roaming eyes threaten to make a meal of you.
You notice how empty they are.

>   *But he is a man of God!*
you argue.
>   *Surely he knows the limits.*
>   *Surely he would never be*
>   *unfaithful…*

And then,
he says,
>   *I promise you'll find God between my legs,*
>   *just give him a little taste.*
He says,
>   *The evil spirits have possessed your*
>   *entire defenseless body.*
>   *Mind if I come say hello?*
He says,
>   *Shh. Stay quiet.*
>   *They won't believe you.*
>   *I am everything here.*

He says so much of nothing
that before long, you have become a shadow
of all his promises. Such a believer
in the scriptures that you fail to see them catch fire
upon escaping his tongue.

You burn again and again in his ashes
until you start to burn in yours too.
And when all is said and done,
there is no God left in this hell,
it's just him and you.
And then
just him.

When the light of your existence is extinguished,
when God's noble face is defiled by his,
and when the lines on the carpet can't keep him in line,
just imagine how many victims will never call themselves survivors.
Just imagine the sincerity of her prayers
being destroyed by the hands of those who she confessed her sins to.
Just imagine hijacking someone's yearning for God, and calling it preaching
call it,
   This is just how men are.
call it,
   We should never discuss someone else's sins.
Call it anything but abuse
     or violence
       or damnation.

And they wonder why faith is hard to come by these days.
What does right, wrong and ritual really mean if a select few are exempt?
Do you ever wonder how the prophets will look at them on judgment day?
Do you know what God says about forgiving those who hurt people,
and then what He says about hypocrites?

   Radical feminist imam hunters,
they dare to call
those of us who hold a mirror up to their faces,
and shed light on their crimes.
There will be no apology
for showing the world
exactly who they are.

So hey,
don't shoot the messengers.

We
are already
wounded
enough.

A List of Ways Oppressors Use God's Name To Further Their Own Agenda

1. A young woman in Madinah sits on the cold marble with her mat and prayer beads near the dome of Masjid Al-Nabawi. She is not allowed inside to see the chamber where the Prophet is buried but for twice a day. A man passing by, who doesn't even work there, snatches up her belongings and violently scatters them all over the floor. He screams, *Women are not allowed near the Prophet!* Muslims believe the Prophet has awareness of those who come to visit him. The man walks away satisfied, believing he is doing God's work. He is so focused on prowling for misbehaving women who don't belong there that he doesn't notice the fire beneath his feet.

2. *I'm an imam, I know how to conduct marriages,* he insists to his second, third, and then fourth secret wife. None of the women know of the other's existence. The third is pregnant.

3. The man lashes his whip for the hundredth time on a mother's back for not picking the designated amount of cotton that is required of her fragile hands. *God made the white man better,* he spits out later on his fourth swig of whiskey. His skin is the first thing the angels tear from him when he's laid into his grave.

4. The colonizers destroy more homes in Palestine to create settlements for their own. *We are God's chosen people,* they proclaim. The ghosts of the massacred children live in the walls.

5. *God would not want you to abort your child,* they proclaim, as the 12-year-old mother lays panting with her belly bigger than her frontal lobe. Having this baby will kill her, but God hates women more than he hates unborn babies so obviously she must sacrifice herself. She begins to bleed out. Her body has not grown into woman just yet and the man who raped her knew it. The heartbeat grows faint. It stops eventually. She is told they both belong in hell. She waits for the flames to lick up her tears.

6. *Ya hajjah, you are not allowed to touch the door of the Ka'bah! Ya hajjah, read this pamphlet about how you should dress when visiting the house of Allah! Ya hajjah, Umrah is not a fashion show!* The abaya in question is beige and has three inches of spangles on the edge of the sleeve. The woman is not wearing makeup. Her worship was accepted long before she walked through the gates.

7. The president of a dying empire drops a bomb every eight minutes for the entirety of his rule. Most times, it hits children, innocents, wipes away entire cities from maps. *God bless america!* the men thunder in unison from behind their joysticks. *We killed all the terrorists!* The surviving children emerge from the rubble with tears streaming from the shrapnel in their eyes. Frantically searching for any sign of a family, they come across a crate of guns instead. *Allahu Akbar.*

Pandemic Elegy

The root

When we survive this,
will we remember
how the world ended for us
in a matter of weeks,
while for others the world
had been burning for years?

letters in Arabic

When our loved ones have left us behind,
will we regret how our bodies served as
weapons to annihilate them,
how our laughter and apathy
perished in our throats a few days too late?

for "human"

When we are back to our old ways,
will we ground ourselves
in how kindness (and dissent)
became the way we coped
while our own demons (and leaders)
threatened to suffocate us?

and "to forget"

When we are on the other side,
will we pray to God this hard
in the late hours of the night
begging for things to go back to "normal"

ن + س + ي

despite knowing "normal"
was a façade to begin with?

are the same.

I see the way you violently obliterate your soul with a conviction that you will never need faith. Know that your desire to remain comfortable in darkness is a defense mechanism to my light. A light of hope and beginnings. You weren't made for this kind of defeat and angst. Rather, you were made for submission. Your soul was made to brighten your path there. Come back. Let the slim light of my crescent guide you on your way.

After The Honeymoon Phase: On The Worst Days

It has been three years and the love is quieter now. There is evidence of a normal life. There are pictures and handmade scrapbooks and laundry scattered about. But the feeling of the chase and the breathlessness of the

longing has disappeared into the hole you feel today. You spend hours of the present, with all you thought you wanted, ruminating over the past, mourning how things would never be the same. How you will never again

hear the whispers and relish the secrets only the two of you were in on. How the hair on your arms will never stand on end the way it used to. How your stomach won't lurch when he winks at you now. The butterflies are

gone and you cannot imagine what the future looks like. Why are all the poems about the yearning and not about the commitment. You want to see the poems about afterwards. What happened after you danced in each

other's arms and got past the honeymoon phase and cried together after fighting over the color of the cabinets and decided to sign a paper signing away forever. Seek poems about the quiet. How many of you made it. What

happens after the blood stops pounding in your ears. Were you able to get past the chase. Were you able to consume the silence. You have mastered the art of reading his lips and the curve of his eyebrows. You can complete

the sentences he has barely formed. He knows your favorite ice cream and will buy it each time you fight. He knows how to drag you out of bed on the days you feel terrible and yet. You are still out of sync sometimes. You

will touch the side of his cheek and he will recoil and your world goes up in flames. You will get into a little spat and he drowns in the shame. Everyone keeps saying it is hard. Your therapist keeps telling you it is so much work

so how come no one warned you this would happen. The hole in your stomach has carved a permanent space for itself there but you will smile and laugh and cry in new entanglements and making up will be short and

you will be two adults trying to save yourselves from drowning and wonder how you both ended up being so different than you thought and what do you do with all of that. On days like this it feels like the walls of your gut are

fighting to pull themselves apart but you fought to the end of the earth to get here. So how did you get here. You lean into the crevice of his neck and breathe in the scent of him. It has been three years and it is a little too quiet.

Eyes Of The Party

The older I get,
the more it's confirmed
just how bored I am
by small talk,

how exhausting it is
to compete
for attention.

I have no desire
to beg for my voice to be
heard above others'
or to prove myself
worthy of
belonging.

What's the point?
I have pictures with
people whose names
I don't even remember.
And if pictures are worth
a thousand words,
those words are so hollow
they couldn't even compose
a poem.

Sure –
I'll welcome an intellectual conversation.
But putting my best foot forward
means sitting at a corner table,
sipping my lemonade,
observing the creased foreheads
coupled with plastic smiles
and fishing the crowd
for a poem.

If I'm successful
(and I usually am),
then this
is my idea
of a
party.

A Heavy Prayer

May God burn the arrogance out of me in this life
before I have to scorch for it in the next.

Ameen.

Escape

World Social Work Day
and the first day of spring
fall within the same week
and I think that's no
coincidence.

I've been burying my nose in fantasy
novels to escape reality

because lately reality
has flickered before my eyes
with doubts
and I am not sure why.

I am learning that no matter what,
I will never have it all figured out
and that I have to be okay with this.
I am learning what it means to let go,
trust in the Divine Creator,
and just how deep my desire for control
controls me.

Writing has been really hard lately
not to mention terrifying
but the one thing I think of when
I observe the world around me,
especially my community,
is resilience.

Call me weird
or call me an observer –
but humanity looks most beautiful to me
when we are all in recovery together.

Writing Through The Storm

When I was 15, I wrote the first poem that would later turn into a tsunami of words. I wrote about my pain. And when my own had lessened, I started

to write about the pain around me. It used to be so easy, the way words imprinted themselves so clearly onto my heart, as if God Himself was

speaking to me, for these words were undoubtedly sacred; call them Divine intervention. My heart had always been an open book that I was waiting

for everyone to read. I've always been a writer but I can't always write. And that is the easiest way I know how to say that I've been burned out long

before the fire in my heart extinguished itself. People say that poets carry within them a whole world of pain. As a therapist, I also carry an entire

universe of stories, and I find myself choking – on my tears or my words – I'm not quite sure which. Sometimes, I imagine myself as a vessel. If I were

one, I think I'd be made of wood: thick-rimmed, smooth finish, and deep enough to hold all the world's troubles. I think a lot of us feel this way. I

have spent the last few years listening, transcribing, consoling. Consoling, transcribing, listening. An ongoing oscillation generated by pain, propelled

by tears, my stern always headfirst into the tempest, now but a mundane journey of the reality of the depth of pain around us. Case notes have

turned into poems. Knives against skin have turned into pens boasting victory. Our words are a battleground for everyone else's weaknesses, and

so are our couches. It is nearly impossible for wet wood to catch aflame, but all my resources have run dry, and these stories are setting my soul on

fire. I always say that to be a vessel that carries people's narratives is a blessing until it starts to feel like a burden. And right now, I could give

Atlas a run for his money. When the girl in my therapy room creates a confessional out of her bare hands, tells me she is praying for the first time

in ages, that she found God again on my small leather couch, the wood finish I had solidified myself with all but cracked, and for a moment I was a

poet again. Noah's ark, after all, was a wooden vessel which managed to save all of creation. I hope whatever depth I have carved out of myself can save at least one life. The way everyone keeps digging, I'm sure I'll get there soon. But will anything be left of me? There are days I am so overwhelmed

with everyone's pain that I start to feel hollow. I wonder who will carry mine when the time comes. You can't pour from an empty cup but what

about when yours is overflowing? What happens when carrying their pain along with yours starts to chip away at you? Your tolerance for pain is

ephemeral. An S.O.S. here is literal. Your soul needs saving, but so do many others, and haven't we learned from the people we serve how much easier it

is to jump ship than face the flood? But at the end of the day, I still write. And it is that choice which makes the storm a little less terrifying, the

hurricane a hurdle, the flame still a fire, the tongue always a storyteller, the heart forever a vessel, and you – a guide to someone else's serenity, a voice

of reason, a beholder of passion. And isn't the storm suddenly so beautiful when it comes with a blessing like that?

For all the people:

—————————, —————————, —————————,

whom we clipped away through our growth.
For all the ones who are undeserving of a poem.

Guilt Trip

After his surgery,
my Abba and I talk politics
in his hotel room near the highway.
I have driven three hours to see him.
Since the last time I gave him my opinion –
I mean truly gave it –
my tongue has sharpened.
I'm not much taller
but I know I am just as intelligent
as he always told me I was.

I give him a list of reasons why
whatever political argument he has
at the moment
has holes in it,
and when he finally agrees with me,
13-year-old Sara who used to say,
I just hate politics
roars in approval.

My Abba tells me that guilt trips work best
as he tries to get a relative to speak to him again.
I outline for him all the reasons why that won't work,
even citing my sources just like he taught me.

He tells me I'm wrong
and that he knows better.
10-year-old Sara surfaces and explodes.
I may not be the ideal daughter
but after all, the only model I had
involved shame.

So I sharply remind him who's the social worker
and who's the engineer.
He may know the best thing in his field
but I sure as hell know mine.
He turns his face to the window,
says he doesn't want to argue,
is quiet for a minute,
and then finally,
asks me to elaborate.
He doesn't know the first thing about people
so for the first time in his life,
he asks me to teach him.

But my Abba
remembers all my birthdays and anniversaries
by gifting me Amazon gift cards
(he doesn't know that I've boycotted Amazon
and I appreciate his thoughtfulness too much to tell him).
His love language is making sure my medicine cabinets
are overflowing with bottles of Vitamins D3 and Zinc.
He stands 40 minutes in line to vote,
then calls me and tells me he did
just to make sure I know.

So after our tumultuous years of angry silence
and then relearning how to speak to each other,
the thing I am most thankful to my Abba for
is reminding me how much my voice matters.
Even in standing up
to him.

Things I Say To Convince Myself I Can't Be Anything But A Poet

It was written in the heavens before I was even born.
How could one big question mark like me be anything else?
On January 1, 2009, I made a New Year's goal to write a book,
and here I am, two down and a lifetime to go.

I've been told my verses stir hearts to life and keep them warm
even on nights when I am wrapped in my own chill.
What a blessing to hold the torch for someone else's comfort
even when you can't quite feel that heat yourself.

When the words come spilling out all over this blank canvas,
my fingers type with an urgency I didn't know existed
(yes, on the Notes app and what about it).
I savor rhymes between my lips to see if they fit just right.
I'm in so deep, I often forget the feel of the final flourish.
So what if I sometimes inch with guilt toward my thesaurus?
The reader will likely thank me for it
as they should.

My therapist tells me I am a badass
disguised in cute packaging and she's right –
a hundred and five pounds with sixty-two inches
of an explosion nobody ever seems to expect.
I don't wear makeup often but when I do my eyeliner
is so sharp, it can cut clean through your bakwaas
and turn it into a really good poem.

As someone who daydreams about setting
everything on fire I am told not to "stir the pot,"
but don't you know that if what's within sits stagnant
for too long the bottom will burn, also known as:
the most vulnerable part will swallow itself whole.

So lend me the longest matchstick you can find.
Set all these pages on fire with an intentional revolution.
My silence is burning a hole in my tongue I no longer welcome.
Picasso said to "learn the rules like a pro so you can break them
like an artist" and I am punching through them all now.
The kaleidoscope of conundrums falls around me like ash.
I feel the Divine gently nudging me away
from the shame. What is poetry, after all,
if not worship?
And what is worship if clouded by doubt?

Legacy

I once lost my voice
for two whole weeks.

There was no fever,
no other symptoms,
just a switch that had been turned off,
like a test within a tragedy.

Why does it take losing a blessing
to remember what a gift it is?

I never doubted its power after this
and I promised to continue using it for good.

Women like me have already been choking
on our own tongue for generations.
Those on the outside mock us for being too silent.
The ones on the inside hate us for being too vocal.

Never again will you see me watering myself down
to make the truth easier to
swallow.

Planting Seeds

When I was seven,
upon hearing that my family was to be uprooted
for the third time in my life across the country,
my farewell rebellion to my little Ohio suburban home
was to do the opposite –
to plant what I hoped would become
an apple tree.

A few brown seeds of the last apple I ate
went into a hole in our flower bed I dug
with my grubby little hands,
desperate to return one day and discover quite literally,
the fruits of my "labor."
But at seven,
I knew nothing about gardening,
nothing about the proportion of sun to soil to water
and certainly nothing about
patience.

Yet, the hope I had that it would blossom
is something I think we could extract.
Something we could make the sweetest nectar from.
Something to make us pause for a moment and drink in the innocence.
The simplicity.
Go back to the basics.
Go back to the possibility – no, the certainty – that planting a seed
can and will create a new and better world.

So tell me, what hopes did you have for your world at seven years old?
Did you dream about planting seeds of your own?
Did you tend to your own gardens of promises
beneath which rivers flowed?
What trees were you forced to leave behind
but naively trusted to bloom in your absence?

When was it that you or a loved one were plucked
from this innocence
like weeds?
Which of you had to withstand the unimaginable
for your naïveté to combust?
What news story was it that lit the first match beneath you?
How old were you when you started fanning the flames
of your own personal fire?
How many hearts did you leave kindled

on your path to justice?
Which of this world's most horrible abominations
did you put a torch to?

More importantly,
at what point did that fire engulf you?
When did you hope to find yourself in the thick of the blaze
only to lose yourself in the darkness?
How deep were you in the inferno
before the heat burned you up and burned you out?

Listen,
I've written a lot of poems about rage and fire
and the anger required to tackle the monsters we only thought
would haunt us in our dreams.
I too have fought and cried and tried to wake up
but found myself on the front lines, on the phone, online, with the leaders,
the lava cooking me alive, and I too
have daydreamed about what the world would look like
if we burned it all down and started over.
I too have burnt up my last flickering candle,
romanced by the poetry of the destruction,
the hypnotic dance of the flame,
eager to warm up my cold heart,
striving to feel something besides despair.

And yet, there's a reason "burnout" contains the word "burn."
There's a reason fire only takes us so far.
When we are left with a colossal pile of ashes and charred remains,
asking "now what?",
know that it is not fire that will create a new world,
but water.
Because even after the Great Flood,
a dove still returned to Noah's ark with
an olive branch.

Did you know that as babies,
water makes up 78% of our bodies,
dropping to 65% by the time we reach our first birthday?
Maybe that explains why we are so full of life as children.
So full of virtue.
What a gift that the answer has been gushing within us this whole time.
That the sea, ebbing and flowing within our very bodies
has given us a lesson in balance from the moment we were born.
Did you know that water asserted its dominance on this planet
millions of years before fire ever could?

Did you know the reason you can see the Grand Canyon from space
is because a persistent ocean now long gone
knew it could literally change the world?
Water is the most versatile thing to ever exist.
It is the only major substance that can take on all three forms of matter.
Adapt to its environment.
No need for it here?
It will evaporate and bless the gift of itself
somewhere else in the world.
Too cold and it will work to preserve its freshness by transforming to ice.
It can destroy just as well as it sculpts.
It can house life and in the same breath,
erode it.
Water quenches the fire but doesn't stop there,
but nourishes,
pours into,
protects,
grows,
rebuilds.

So go ahead –
rise up, but do it like an ocean wave;
go crashing down only to come right back.
Erode those systemic barriers but be a monsoon;
shower them with so much of your rage but leave flowers
and budding crops in the process.
Safeguard your people with a fury,
but be like the glaciers,
which loved freshwater so much they have been calmly rock solid
to protect it for thousands of years.
Be like the water that baptizes a baby,
that purifies a Muslim five times a day before prayer.
Moses may not be here to split the Red Sea anymore
but the pharaohs of our time without a doubt will drown —
in our love.

And what world
could we create if we all watered
our own little apple trees?
If we didn't abandon them to chase the fire but instead nourished them?
There is nothing more exhilarating than uprooting the walls
but there is nothing more rewarding than cultivating the bridges.
No evil is greater than the Divine power of our love.
And perhaps changing the world is too big an ambition,
but there are endless possibilities
when planting new seeds.

The Poems Are Longer Now

These days, I can no longer condense the complex
concepts that formulate my thoughts into small and
short verses; now that I've arrived here, I wonder

why it took me this long. I have desperately been
trying to find myself in the words again and felt a
deep sense of betrayal when I thought they left me.

In reality, they have always been there. I have been
the one guilty of deserting them. I have been so
terrified of what may spill out that I've just been

busy trying to reel it all in. I have beat myself up
over how silly they may sound leaving my mouth
or my pen or my mind instead of just letting them

leave. What a disservice to myself I've committed
because of fear. What a tragedy indeed. These days,
when I write a new poem, my entire body trembles

and quakes. You can't convince me the Divine doesn't
have a hand in these revelations. That the mountains
don't shudder upon a poet's endless rebirthing.

Birthday Surprises Pt. III

i. When I turned 27, I got three juicers in the mail, the kind of water bottle that doesn't shatter or leak and a Hagrid birthday cake. When my husband and I moved into our first apartment together, fresh banana pudding from Magnolia Bakery had been mailed all the way from New York. Later, I came home to a plant on my doorstep that grew to become my favorite, all of which is to say my friends know me very well. I am 28 now and these bonds feel like sunbeams. No obligations, no unspoken expectations and we have added voice notes and complicated recipes to the list of love languages. The difference between a long drive and time well spent is a three-hour catch-up call where we cover everything from the weather to your IBS to the weird place your patient stuck something to the last words your father spoke to you before he died. I write poems with some friends on Wednesdays and there are others who mail me cookies from another state, sometimes even homemade. Another friend who lives 10 minutes away composes a new calligraphy piece each time we meet and it's true what they say, that best friends see each other four times a year and have no pictures together because I have about four pieces per each year of our friendship and our contact photos for each other are truly not aging well.

ii. Once, before I understood what performance poetry was, I stood up on a stage and gave my first TEDx talk and it was a big deal but none of my friends came. Once, there was a time when my biggest cheerleaders were people I only knew online. Once, I was mocked for being too busy to hang out when all I did in my free time was sleep and eat (that's a lie, I didn't have free time). Once, the fear in my eyes at the expensive restaurant they insisted we go to was a foreign language even the waiter understood. Once, the night before my Biostatistics final, a best friend broke up with me in a way that was so out of left field I couldn't even standard error of measurement my way out of failing the next day. I remember actually wanting to die and I thought only romance gone wrong could make you feel like that. I have become well-acquainted with the "unfollow" and "unfriend" buttons - yes even on Venmo - and there are names and faces littered throughout scrapbooks and albums who are chapters long closed.

iii. Hell, I know I'm not perfect and I have dished out my fair share of hurt. But wow, if you and I can get in a spat in the kitchen, or if I accidentally shrink your laundry and we can laugh about it 30 minutes later, or if getting defensive isn't part of the story for a hard conversation, and if you aren't really a poetry person but will read everything I write from beginning to end, and if your prayers include my name in them, I know we'll be just fine.

iv. Once, I used to hate birthdays but I think that's because I didn't know what it meant to be loved right by the people around me.

Surprise.

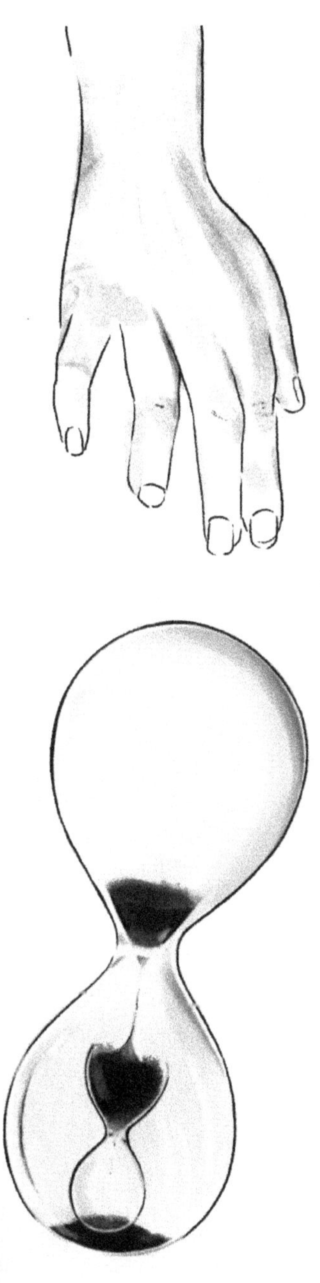

Notes

- A previous version of this book was longlisted for Button Poetry's 2021 Annual Chapbook Contest.

- "Quarantine Meditation" on page 36 was written in one of Rupi Kaur's pandemic workshops.

- Different versions of "For Dark-Skinned Girls" on page 27 and "End Of Days" on pages 54-55 were originally published in Gival Press's Arlington Literary Journal, Issue 166a.

- "Quarter Life Crisis" on pages 50-51 was written after Rudy Francisco's "My Honest Poem."

- "A Response To 'You're A Little Too Radical'" on page 53 was originally aired on the "What Radicalized You" podcast, episode 63: "I can't therapy away some of these problems."

- "Pandemic Elegy" on page 63 was written after Laura Kelly Fanucci.

- "Planting Seeds" on pages 76-78 was a commissioned project by the American Civil Liberties Union of Texas and originally aired as a spoken word piece.

Acknowledgments

This book has been a labor of love for nearly 5 years. All praises are first and foremost for Allah, who has blessed my life immensely with the support and love that was needed to finish this book. This was a spiritual project as equally as it was an artistic one and I pray it is accepted by Him.

My wonderful early editors including Amal Kassir, Sadiyah Bashir, and Isra Cheema, who are outstanding poets as well as friends, helped me see things I did not in my own work. The concept and heart of this book was born in one of Amal's writing workshops, which is so fitting. Thank you to my later editors, SG Huerta, as well as Suzi Q. Smith, who was also an earlier reader of this work and critiqued both earlier and later versions of this manuscript with grace and compassion. Thank you to others who also helped revise earlier versions of this manuscript including Bilal Moon, Vogue Robinson, Lindsay Maroney, and Rocio Franco.

Thank you to my beta readers Batool Chaudhry, Gabriela Aguilar, Aiysha Alamgir, Shandraya Asante, and Irum Ibrahim – all dear friends and incredible artists themselves – who held my work with care and annotated rigorously to give me the feedback I needed. Thank you also to Kashmir Maryam, Marjan Naderi, and Raef Haggag for your generous reading of this book.

I am incredibly grateful for my wonderful illustrator Afeefah Khazi-Syed, a gifted poet as well, who I met through an editing project, and who blew me away with bringing my work to life. Adding illustrations to this book was an experimental endeavor and her pieces made it so worth it.

A huge acknowledgment to other creatives and artist friends including Muhaajir Sayer, F.S. Yousaf, and Alia Salem for holding space and being wonderful cheerleaders. And a major thank you to my friends Fatima Ahmad, Hiba Alkhadra, Kainat Hamid, Hiba Fatima, Amina Choudhury, and Humna Tariq for their endless encouragement.

To my family: my husband, Usama Malik, who generously provided time and expertise for the cover design for both books, your selflessness and willingness to give means more than you could know. To my mother Sabina Ibraheem, my sister Aisha Bawany, and my mother-in-law and her sister, Amatus Sami Yasmin and Amatur Rafiq – you all are some of the best women I know and my life and art is endlessly inspired by you.

A major thank you to Zainab Yoonas who kindly critiqued this manuscript from an Islamic perspective. Any mistake I have made despite her feedback is entirely my own and not to be attributed to any oversight on her part.

Thank you to Erik Martínez Resly from ACLU Texas, who commissioned me for "Planting Seeds," and in effect, solidified the final missing puzzle piece that was added to this book.

Thank you to 3rd Culture Collective, Generaction Jam, Malikah, House of Amal, FACE, Performing Arts Mosaic and countless other organizations and initiatives that gave many of the poems in this book a platform for the first time, and consequently, readers, listeners, and friends.

I am deeply grateful for the team at FlowerSong Press, especially Edward Vidaurre, who believed in and embraced this project enough to create a permanent home for it.

There are too many to name but a huge thank you to fellow MFA poetry students and professors at Texas State University, who viewed a few of these poems in workshop as I turned something in out of desperation and emerged with a clearer direction of where to take them next. I'm so grateful to be in community with and am always in awe of all of you.

I would be remiss if I did not thank Naomi Shihab Nye, a dear professor and mentor, who guided me toward the best version of this book with her sharp wisdom and ability to gently correct my mental blocks. I finally understand the patience you ushered me to hold on to and this book became a much better version of itself under the guidance you gave me.

To my entire community, to everyone who has been there since the beginning during the Facebook notes, Instagram poetry and self-publishing days, holding my first book with so much love and sticking around despite the major changes both I and my work went through – there are too many of you to name, but this book was possible because of you. Poetry, after all, is strongest when shared with community.

About The Author

Sara Bawany is an award-winning published poet, freelance editor, and licensed clinical social worker. She is a Master of Fine Arts in Creative Writing candidate at Texas State University with a concentration in poetry, previously graduating from The University of Texas at Austin with her Master's in Social Work. Sara is a practicing therapist and serves as the Director of Case Management at Facing Abuse in Community Environments (FACE), an organization that aims to create culture change around leadership abuse in the Muslim community.

Sara began sharing her work publicly in 2016, garnering several thousand readers, and she published her first book in September 2018, titled: *(w)holehearted: a collection of poetry and prose*, which won Daybreak Press Publishing's 2019 "Best Poetry Book" award. She was also selected as a finalist in Button Poetry's 2021 Annual Chapbook Contest. Her work has been featured twice on TEDx, ACLU Texas, 99 Clay Vessels: The Muslim Women Storytelling Project, Arlington Literary Journal, Vision Magazine, Muslim Youth Musings, and Brown Girl Magazine. She has spoken, taught, and performed at more than 100 different engagements both in her social work capacity and as a poet. *Quarter Life Crisis* is her second book.

Sara is the Assistant Managing Editor at Porter House Review, and a volunteer reader at Abode Press. She has a small freelance editing business that aims to empower and strengthen writers who seek her assistance. She serves as a senior mentor and Process Manager at House of Amal, a small writing institution that empowers and supports young Muslim writers. You can access her work at www.sarabawany.com, and on Facebook, Instagram, and TikTok (@sara.bawany).

About The Illustrator

Afeefah Khazi-Syed was born and raised in the DFW metroplex but has always called two places home: the suburbs of Texas and her grandparents' homes in Southern India. Medical student by day, poet and illustrator by night, Afeefah finds joy in unraveling stories in the people and world around her. In 2022, she published her first poems in the anthology: *Our Ancestors Did Not Breathe This Air.*